HOW TO PLAY TEXAS HOLD'EM POKER

Summersdale Publishers Ltd
46 West Street
Chichester
West Sussex
PO19 1RP
UK

www.summersdale.com

Printed and bound in Belgium

ISBN 1 84024 511 5

HOW TO PLAY

THE GAME PLAYED ON INTERNET POKER SITES

TEXAS HOLD'EM

PROBABLY THE MOST POPULAR
FORM OF POKER IN THE WORLD,
TEXAS HOLD'EM IS PLAYED IN MOST
OF THE WORLD'S TOP COMPETITIONS
AND INTERNET POKER SITES.

IN THIS BOOK YOU WILL LEARN
ALL THE BASICS OF HOW TO PLAY
RIGHT THROUGH TO HOW TO BET
AND BLUFF PROPERLY.

CONTENTS

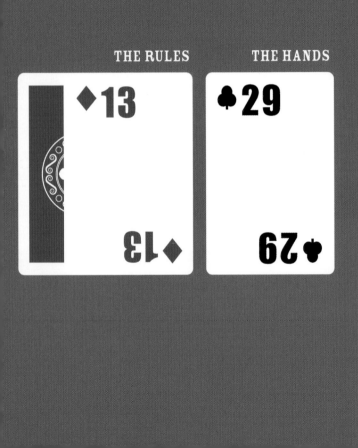

THE RULES

♦13

THE HANDS

♣29

THE RULES

HOW TO WIN :

A HAND CAN BE WON EITHER WITH
THE BEST FIVE-CARD COMBINATION

OR BY MAKING YOUR OPPONENTS
THROW IN THEIR CARDS.

EACH PLAYER IS DEALT TWO CARDS FACE DOWN.

THESE ARE KNOWN AS THE 'HOLE' OR 'POCKET' CARDS. THE HOLE CARDS ARE NOT REVEALED TO THE OTHER PLAYERS UNTIL THE BETTING IS FINALLY CALLED.

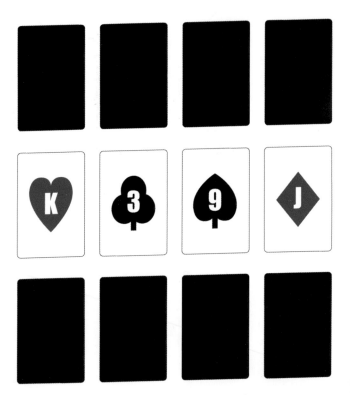

FIVE CARDS ARE DEALT FACE
UP IN THE CENTRE OF THE TABLE.
THESE ARE THE 'COMMUNITY CARDS'
AND ARE SHARED BY ALL PLAYERS.
THE WINNER IS DETERMINED BY
THE BEST FIVE-CARD COMBINATION
FROM THESE SEVEN CARDS.

ORDER OF PLAY :

1.

THE DEALER GIVES EACH PLAYER
THEIR OWN TWO CARDS FACE DOWN.

THIS IS FOLLOWED BY THE FIRST
ROUND OF BETTING.

2.

THE DEALER REMOVES THE TOP CARD, KNOWN AS BURNING A CARD, THEN DEALS THREE COMMUNITY CARDS FACE UP.

THIS IS KNOWN AS 'THE FLOP'.

IT IS FOLLOWED BY THE SECOND ROUND OF BETTING.

3.

THE DEALER BURNS ANOTHER
CARD AND DEALS ONE MORE
COMMUNITY CARD.

THIS IS KNOWN AS 'THE TURN'.

IT IS FOLLOWED BY THE THIRD
ROUND OF BETTING.

4.

THE DEALER THEN BURNS ONE MORE CARD FOLLOWED BY THE FINAL COMMUNITY CARD.

THIS IS KNOWN AS 'THE RIVER'.

THERE IS THEN A FOURTH AND FINAL ROUND OF BETTING.

5.

ONCE THE BETTING HAS ENDED ALL REMAINING PLAYERS REVEAL THEIR CARDS STARTING WITH THE LAST PERSON TO RAISE THE BET.

THIS IS KNOWN AS 'THE SHOWDOWN'.

IF ALL BUT ONE PLAYER FOLDS THEN THE REMAINING PLAYER CAN CLAIM THE POT WITHOUT EVER HAVING TO REVEAL THEIR HAND.

IN TEXAS HOLD'EM THE DEALER IS
DETERMINED BY THE DEALER BUTTON.
THE DEALER BUTTON MOVES AROUND
THE TABLE CLOCKWISE AT THE END OF
EACH HAND, GIVING EVERYBODY THE
CHANCE TO DEAL.

IN COMPETITIONS AND ONLINE GAMES
THIS JOB IS TAKEN ON BY A DESIGNATED
DEALER, BUT THE DEALER BUTTON IS
STILL USED IN ORDER TO DETERMINE
WHO STARTS THE BETTING.

BURN

THE PROCESS OF REMOVING THE
TOP CARD - OR BURNING A CARD,
AS IT IS BETTER KNOWN - IS DONE
TO STOP CHEATING IN CASE
ANYBODY HAPPENS TO CATCH
A GLIMPSE OF THE REMAINING TOP
CARD FROM THE PREVIOUS DEAL.

AT THE BEGINNING OF THE GAME AND
BEFORE EACH HAND THE DEALER
SHUFFLES THE DECK.

WHAT BEATS ?WHAT

ROYAL FLUSH

STRAIGHT FLUSH

FOUR OF A KIND

FULL HOUSE

FLUSH

STRAIGHT

THREE OF A KIND

TWO PAIR

PAIR

ACE HIGH

THE HANDS

KNOW WHAT YOU'VE GOT

NOW THAT YOU KNOW THE RULES, IT'S TIME TO LEARN THE DIFFERENCE BETWEEN A STRAIGHT, A FLUSH AND A STRAIGHT FLUSH.

ROYAL FLUSH

ace, king, queen, jack, ten of the same suit

A ROYAL FLUSH IS THE BEST POSSIBLE HAND YOU CAN MAKE. IF YOU MANAGE TO DRAW THIS HAND YOU CAN'T LOSE!

UNFORTUNATELY THE ODDS OF MAKING THIS HAND ON THE FLOP ARE ALMOST 20,000/1.

BUT DON'T WORRY, THERE ARE PLENTY OF OTHER HANDS YOU CAN MAKE ...

STRAIGHT

any five numerically consecutive numbers of the same suit

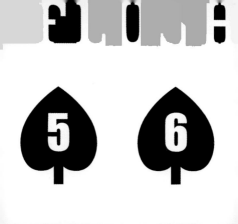

any four cards of
the same value

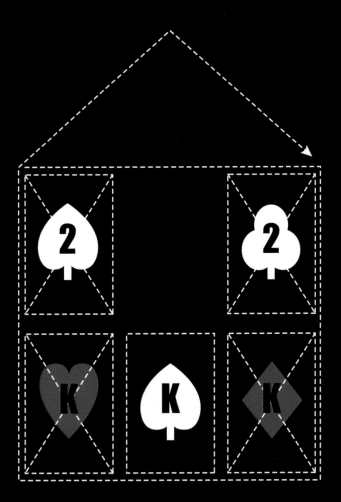

38

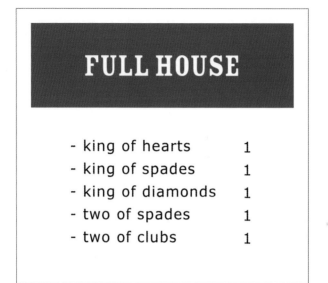

FULL HOUSE

- king of hearts	1
- king of spades	1
- king of diamonds	1
- two of spades	1
- two of clubs	1

Three cards of one value plus two of another. The highest ranking trio determines the winner when multiple hands occur.

any five cards
of the same suit

STRAIGHT

five numerically consecutive numbers of any suit

OF A KIND

three cards of the same
numerical value

TWO

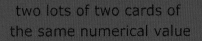

two lots of two cards of
the same numerical value

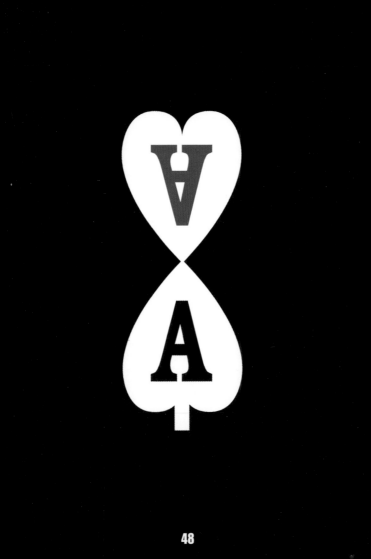

PAIR

two cards of the same numerical value

HIGH

when no hand can be made the highest card wins

THE BETTING

BETTING

UNLIKE MOST FORMS OF GAMBLING, WHERE BETTING IS MADE ON THE PARTICULAR OUTCOME OF A GAME, BETTING IN POKER IS AN INTEGRAL PART OF THE GAME ITSELF. IT ADDS THE ELEMENT OF SKILL TO WHAT WOULD OTHERWISE BE A GAME OF JUST CHANCE.

WITH TEXAS HOLD'EM THERE IS NO ANTE. INSTEAD THERE IS WHAT IS KNOWN AS 'THE BLINDS'.

THE PLAYER TO THE IMMEDIATE LEFT OF THE DEALER PUTS IN THE 'SMALL BLIND' (1/2 THE MINIMUM BET) AND THE NEXT PLAYER TO HIS LEFT PUTS IN THE 'BIG BLIND' (EQUIVALENT TO THE FULL MINIMUM BET). THE BLINDS ARE PUT IN AT THE START OF EVERY HAND.

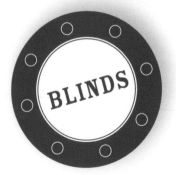

IN THE FIRST ROUND OF BETTING (BEFORE THE FLOP) THE PLAYER TO THE LEFT OF THE TWO BLINDS STARTS THE BETTING. THEY CAN EITHER CALL, FOLD OR RAISE. IF THEY CALL THEY HAVE TO MATCH THE BIG BLIND.

IN ALL SUBSEQUENT ROUNDS (AFTER
THE FLOP) IT IS THE FIRST PLAYER
TO THE DEALER'S LEFT THAT STARTS
THE BETTING. THEY CAN RAISE, FOLD
OR CHECK. IF THEY RAISE THEY CAN
BET AS MUCH AS THEY LIKE, UNLESS
THERE IS A LIMIT. ALL SUBSEQUENT
PLAYERS THEN EITHER HAVE TO CALL,
RAISE AGAIN OR FOLD.

IF THE FIRST PLAYER CHECKS IT MEANS THEY OFFER NO BET AT ALL. IF ALL SUBSEQUENT PLAYERS CHOOSE TO CHECK THEN THE BETTING MOVES ON TO THE NEXT ROUND.

FOLDING IS WHEN A PLAYER THROWS IN THEIR HAND.

CALLING IS WHEN SOMEONE MATCHES THE PREVIOUS BET.

IF A PLAYER GOES ALL IN, THEY PLACE ALL THEIR REMAINING CHIPS INTO THE POT. OTHER PLAYERS CANNOT RAISE ABOVE THIS BET BUT CAN ONLY MATCH IT.

HOWEVER, IF THERE IS MORE THAN ONE OTHER PLAYER LEFT IN THE GAME, THEY CAN CONTINUE TO RAISE THE BETTING IN A SEPARATE POT.

IF THE PLAYER WHO HAS GONE ALL IN EVENTUALLY WINS THE HAND, THEY DO NOT TAKE ANYTHING FROM THIS SEPARATE POT. INSTEAD IT IS SPLIT BETWEEN THE REMAINING PLAYERS.

ROUND OF BETTING
(EXAMPLE OF BETTING BEFORE THE FLOP)

PLAYER 3
(SMALL BLIND)

PLAYER 4
(BIG BLIND)

PLAYER 5 - CALL
(PUTS IN 1)

PLAYER 1 - CALL
(PUTS IN 1)

PLAYER 2 - FOLD
(PUTS IN 0)

PLAYER 3 - CALL
(HAVING ALREADY POSTED THE SMALL BLIND,
PLAYER 3 ONLY NEEDS TO PUT IN 1/2 TO MATCH
EVERYBODY ELSE'S BET)

PLAYER 4 - CHECK
(AS THERE IS NO RAISE, PLAYER 4 CAN CHOOSE
NOT TO PUT ANY MORE INTO THE POT)

PLAYER 1.

  PLAYER 2.

 PLAYER 3.

PLAYER 4.

PLAYER 5.

ROUND OF BETTING
(EXAMPLE OF BETTING AFTER THE FLOP)

PLAYER 3 - RAISE 1
(PUTS IN 1)

PLAYER 4 - SEE YOUR 1, RAISE 2
(PUTS IN 3)

PLAYER 5 - FOLD
(PUTS IN 0)

PLAYER 1 - SEE YOUR 2, RAISE 2
(PUTS IN 5)

PLAYER 3 - FOLD
(PUTS IN 0)

PLAYER 4 - CALL
(PUTS IN 2)

PLAYER 1.

D

(PLAYER 2.)

PLAYER 3.

PLAYER 4.

PLAYER 5.

WINNING HAND

EXAMPLE 1:

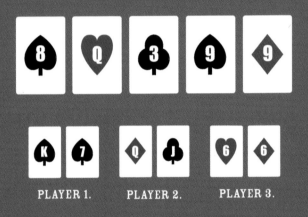

PLAYER 1.   PLAYER 2.   PLAYER 3.

LET'S HAVE A LOOK AT WHO WOULD WIN
THE POT IN A SHOWDOWN.

PLAYER 1 ONLY HAS A KING HIGH.
WITH TWO SPADES HE WAS PROBABLY
HOPING FOR A FLUSH.

PLAYER 2 AND 3 BOTH HAVE TWO PAIRS.

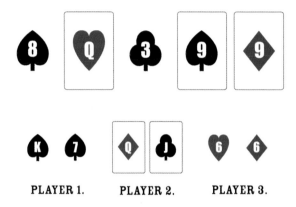

PLAYER 1.   PLAYER 2.   PLAYER 3.

HOWEVER, DESPITE BOTH PLAYER 2
AND PLAYER 3 HOLDING A TWO-PAIR
HAND, IT IS PLAYER 2 WHO WINS.

THIS IS BECAUSE PLAYER 2 HOLDS A
HIGHER PAIR IN HIS HAND WITH THE
PAIR OF QUEENS.

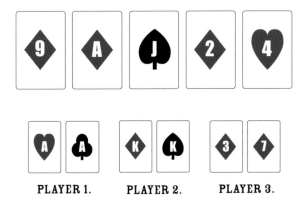

PLAYER 1.   PLAYER 2.   PLAYER 3.

IN THIS EXAMPLE BOTH PLAYER 1 AND
PLAYER 2 START WITH STRONG PAIRS.

PLAYER 1 THEN STRENGTHENS HIS
HAND FURTHER BY DRAWING A THIRD
ACE ON THE FLOP.

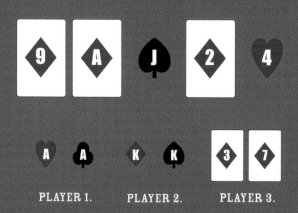

PLAYER 1.   PLAYER 2.   PLAYER 3.

BUT IT IS PLAYER 3 WHO EVENTUALLY
HOLDS THE WINNING HAND.

STARTING WITH THE WEAKEST OF ALL
THE HOLE CARDS, PLAYER 3 CRUISES
INTO POLE POSITION WHEN DRAWING
A FLUSH ON THE TURN.

SPLIT POT

EXAMPLE 1:

PLAYER 1.　　　PLAYER 2.

SOMETIMES YOU DON'T NEED TO USE
BOTH CARDS TO FORM THE BEST HAND.

WHO HAS THE WINNING HAND ABOVE?

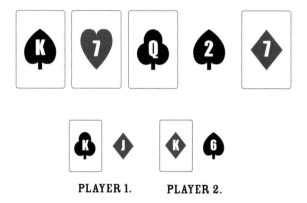

PLAYER 1.   PLAYER 2.

BOTH HAVE THE SAME HAND BECAUSE
THE BEST FIVE CARDS TO BE MADE
FROM THE SEVEN ARE: K K 7 7 Q.

BOTH USE THE KING BUT THEIR OTHER
CARD IS NOT NEEDED. AS THEY BOTH
EFFECTIVELY HAVE THE SAME HAND
THE POT IS SPLIT.

EXAMPLE 2:

PLAYER 1. PLAYER 2.

ON RARE OCCASIONS YOU DON'T NEED
TO USE EITHER OF YOUR TWO HOLE
CARDS TO FORM THE BEST FIVE-CARD
COMBINATION.

PLAYER 1.   PLAYER 2.

IN THIS EXAMPLE WE SEE THAT THE
BEST FIVE-CARD COMBINATION DOES
NOT INCLUDE ANY OF THE PLAYERS'
HOLE CARDS AND IS MADE UP ENTIRELY
OF THE FIVE COMMUNITY CARDS.

ONCE AGAIN THE POT IS SPLIT.

BLUFFING

POKER IS A GAME OF LUCK AND SKILL.
LUCK IN THE HAND YOU ARE DEALT
AND SKILL IN THE WAY THAT YOU BET.

YOU CAN WIN EVEN WHEN YOU HAVE AN
INFERIOR HAND
TO YOUR OPPONENT'S.

THIS IS ACHIEVED BY BETTING AS IF
YOU HAVE A SUPERIOR HAND AND IS
KNOWN AS BLUFFING.

YOU CAN ALSO BLUFF WHEN YOU HAVE
A GOOD HAND.

WHEN BLUFFING WITH A WEAK HAND
YOU ARE LOOKING TO FORCE YOUR
OPPONENTS TO FOLD THEIRS.
SO RAISE BIG AND DON'T HESITATE.

WHEN YOU HAVE A STRONG HAND YOU
ARE LOOKING TO ENTICE AS MUCH
MONEY FROM YOUR OPPONENT AS
POSSIBLE. SO HESITATION IS NOT
NECESSARILY A BAD THING.

YOU CAN BET SMALL TO START WITH,
DRAWING THEM IN, THEN ONCE THEY
HAVE TAKEN THE BAIT YOU CAN RAISE
THE BET TO SOMETHING MORE COSTLY.

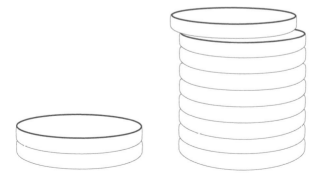

SOMETIMES IT CAN BE A GOOD IDEA
TO LET PEOPLE KNOW WHEN YOU
HAVE BEEN BLUFFING. THAT WAY
WHEN YOU ARE NOT BLUFFING THEY
MAY GET CAUGHT OUT.

TRY TO VARY YOUR PLAY. BLUFFING
TOO OFTEN WILL MAKE YOUR GAME
OBVIOUS AND PREDICTABLE. THIS IS
A DANGEROUS THING AS OTHER
PLAYERS WILL BE ABLE TO READ YOU
MORE EASILY AND EXPLOIT THIS FACT.
SO TO BE MOST SUCCESSFUL WHEN
BLUFFING, USE OCCASIONALLY.

SPOTTING THE BLUFF

IT IS ALWAYS WORTH STUDYING YOUR OPPONENTS, ESPECIALLY WHEN YOU ARE OUT OF A HAND. WATCH TO SEE IF THEY HAVE ANY NERVOUS TICKS OR STRANGE MANNERISMS.

THE LONGER THE GAME GOES ON THE BETTER YOU SHOULD GET TO KNOW YOUR OPPONENTS' PLAY.

OBVIOUSLY YOU CANNOT DO THIS ONLINE, INSTEAD, TRY TO WATCH OUT FOR REPEAT BETTING PATTERNS.

OTHER TIPS :

THERE'S NO SHAME IN FOLDING.
A DISCIPLINED BETTING STYLE
WILL STAND YOU IN MUCH BETTER
STEAD THAN A WILD ONE. SO PLAY
TIGHT AND BET ON A FEW HANDS
RATHER THAN EVERY ONE.

IF THE BETTING STAYS LOW IN THE
FIRST ROUND, EVEN IF YOU HAVE WHAT
LOOKS LIKE A VERY POOR HAND, IT'S
SOMETIMES WORTH STAYING IN TO SEE
WHAT COMES UP IN THE FLOP.

PERHAPS THE BIGGEST THING TO
REMEMBER IS THAT THE COMMUNITY
CARDS ARE SHARED BY YOU AND
EVERY OTHER PLAYER. GET INTO THE
HABIT OF THINKING ABOUT WHAT
THEY MIGHT MEAN, NOT ONLY TO YOU
BUT ALSO YOUR OPPONENTS.

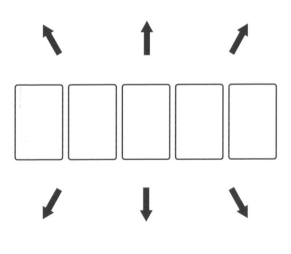

DON'T PAY TOO MUCH ATTENTION
TO TIPS IN BOOKS.

NOW THAT YOU KNOW HOW TO PLAY
TEXAS HOLD'EM, THE BEST WAY TO
IMPROVE YOUR GAME IS TO PLAY.

NOW THAT YOU KNOW HOW TO PLAY
THE GAME ALL YOU NEED IS A BUNCH
OF MATES, A PACK OF CARDS AND
SOME CHIPS. GOOD LUCK.

1.

2.

3.

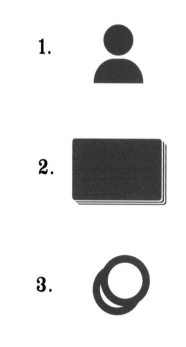

mixed nuts

other books by MikWright, Ltd.

hey, girl!

happy birthday . . . blah, blah, blah

who's your daddy?

your mother looks good . . .

MikWright . . . family style

drinks well with others

mixed nuts

MikWright

Andrews McMeel
Publishing

Kansas City

mixed nuts

04 05 06 07 08 TWP 10 9 8 7 6 5 4 3 2 1

ISBN: 0-7404-4748-7

www.mikwright.com

book composition by kelly & company, lee's summit, missouri

———————— attention: schools and businesses ————————

Andrews McMeel books are available at quantity
discounts with bulk purchase for educational, business,
or sales promotional use. For information, please write to:
Special Sales Department, Andrews McMeel Publishing,
4520 Main Street, Kansas City, Missouri 64111.

we dedicate this book to those of you who can:

—merge in traffic, use a blinker, or both.

—have your deposit slip filled out "before"
you get to the drive-through teller.

—put your cell phone down long enough
to order your latte.

acknowledgments

mixed nuts, in itself, acknowledges that people are not as fully evolved as they would have you believe. take our families for instance. normal to many, koo-koo to others. (for god's sake, mom, throw out the fast-food condiments already!)

why suddenly all the fuss over dysfunction? it's as american as baseball and apple pie. in reality, the family that isn't screwed up is really the dysfunctional one.

kooky or not, we acknowledge the following:

our moms and dads, who have never divorced. (these days, that's dysfunctional.)

tim's uncle, who invented the merry-go-round at kmart.

tim's grandfather, who never stepped foot into a hospital except to die.

mixed nuts

we ended the relationship as
friends. you can e-mail him at
lying-cheating-son-of-a-bitch.com

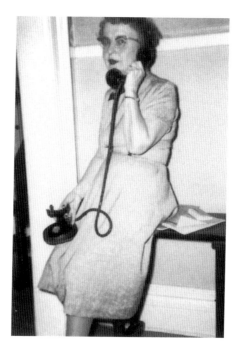

if you can't say something nice
about someone, i want to hear it.

homework stinks!

tonight we have to study uranus.

the salesman was right . . .

what a babe magnet!

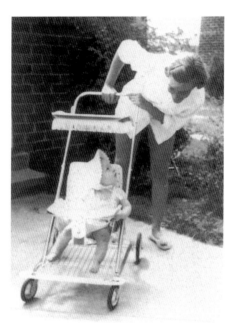

don't worry sweetie, we'll know soon.
the d.n.a. results come back friday.

what a life.

she lets you sleep as late as you want.
hell, she promotes it. then you get a
little nipple and take another nap. soon
she's slapped some powder on your butt
cheeks and it's back to the nipple.

(wait, that was my last date!)

after i got him home i couldn't believe
the size of it.

later i went fishing.

once again, he's thirty minutes late.
i have half a mind to go home
to my sick husband.

honey, don't you worry about getting laid off.
as long as there are sidewalks, you'll always
have a job.

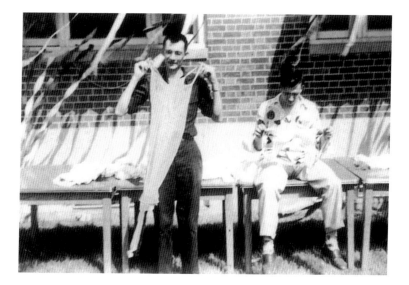

darrell was devastated the day he got his
pink slip. he specifically ordered yellow.

whatever it is . . .

no.

no.

i said no.

but, daaaaad!

no.

if they jumped off a cliff,
would you do that too?

now, you can march right back upstairs
and change that blouse.

and i want you home by nine.

no.

if you think i'm gonna spend another six months cooped up with a bunch of half-naked, sweat-drenched, foul-mouthed strangers . . . you're right!

dear mom,

prison is not so bad after all.
my cell mate, leon, is really nice.

p.s. please send lipstick and a wig.

now that he's gone, i love you best!
but remember, we still haven't
checked the pound.

you know, with everybody getting
laid off, i'm just wondering
when i'm going to get laid on.

someone should have warned
lisa's mother about the pitfalls
of using a discount sperm bank.

oh my god!

nature or nurture?

weren't we all there? . . . metal mouth,
four eyes, hormones, fashion fright.

but, little lisa gets the last laugh
(exclamation point!) today she towers 6'2"
tall, flows like ginger rogers, runs a national
consulting business, mothers a hoard of cats,
makes the best damn martini you've ever sucked
down, *and* totes a darling husband on her wrist
that makes both women and men wince. (bitch!)

if lisa (love her!) made one mistake it's that
she let martha stewart take a page from her life
and turn it into an empire. well, ex-empire.

i don't have anything against your
trailer. hell, i was conceived up
against a double-wide.

from the looks of these skid marks,
it must have been a horrible accident.

not sure what to get me
for christmas?

i could always use a few more
knick-knacks.

got nipple?

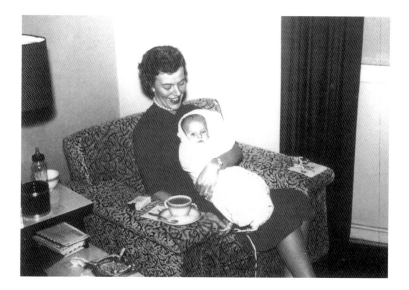

being a mother has been the best experience
of my life. that reminds me . . .
i'm out of prozac.

all this talk about postpartum depression.
of course everybody's depressed!

back in mom's day, politically correct meant
voting for that hunk jfk! a little ciggie,
some kahlua and folgers, and *all my children*
kept our mothers well balanced. the daily
coffee parties were a huge part of the
'60s stay-at-home euphoria. (a little
gossip never hurt anyone, right?)

women weren't expected to be running up
against a glass ceiling. no dashing some
kid to ballet, soccer, piano lessons, and
confirmation classes. no getting the schnauzer
to the vet for a teeth cleaning. no video returns.
no pop-up ads.

admit it, ladies. you'd take your mom's
life as a mother in a heartbeat.
wait, you'd have to use cloth diapers.

never mind. pop a xanax.

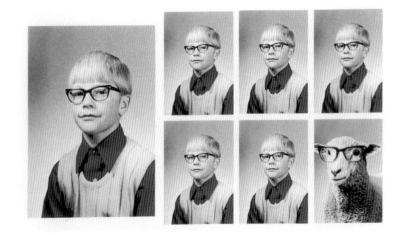

cloning mishap sparks national debate.

fourth grade. tyler, minnesota. poppy poster winner many times over.

i remember wanting wire-rimmed glasses, but dad thought they looked too much like what the "hippies" were wearing on television. (check out the lovely alternative to wire.) as luck would have it, dad later caved in and i got my damn wire-rimmed glasses. well, in the not-so-lucky category, i promptly dove into lake benton with them on and set the farm budget back another sixty bucks. (slick move.)

all in all, i liked the farm. we had fabulous vegetables, scrumptious fresh butter, and big, sweaty farmhands.

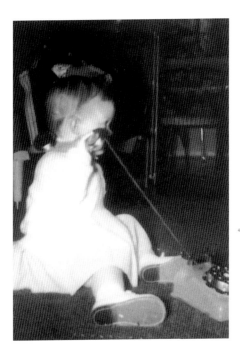

grandma, you gotta get me
out of here! they ran out of
diapers and got me wearing yours!

do i look like a people person?

honest to god, true story . . .

our friend's grandmother was struck by lightning
and lived to tell about it. she was a changed
person, for sure. it was as if the bolt singed
her sense of humor to the point where
everything serious was reason to giggle.
you know . . . someone tripping, car crashes,
twisters and trailers.

aside from minor tragedies,
grandmama rarely smiled.

yes.

for your birthday i'm giving you a
stringer of fish. i know it's not
much, but i heard you already have
a case of crabs.

let's see . . . we'll crawl out of the sack at
five a.m., drive to lake nightmare, stick a
cold worm on a rusty, jagged hook (murder),
toss it in the water and stare at a twenty-
nine-cent fluorescent bobber for six hours.
if we're "lucky" we reel in some slimy, spiny,
mad-as-hell, scale-ridden, fry-pan-bound guppy.
oh, why don't we throw him in a bucket of water
for a few hours while we try for more? what
fun! (picture tobacco spitting and man-type
scratching for full effect.)

can't you just buy fish in the store? you know
they have lots of fresh fish, meats, vegetables,
and bread in warm, well-lit grocery stores from
coast to coast. the kitchen? isn't that the room
where everyone stands during parties?

waiter! i'll have the seared ahi, baby
vegetables, and a glass of 1997 pinot. oh,
could you bring some more tomato-basil-dill
spread, please?

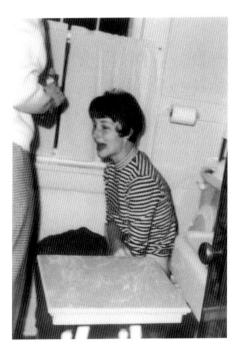

sorry i haven't called.
i've been a little gassy.

think of it like this . . .
in dog years you'd be dead.

hey! remember what you gave me last year for christmas? well, the cream finally cleared it up.

excuse me santa. kent gets a wood-burning
set, a tractor trailer rig, an etch-o-sketch,
blue jeans, and a card game?
well . . . i've been screwed again,
only this time by a stick pony.

the results of your color analysis
are in. you look good in nothing.

mother-in-law edna is allergic to the sun.

edna, quite possibly, makes the best southern
pecan pie ever. her secret? she won't divulge,
but we think she doubles the vanilla.(which you
will find in the cellar along with sixteen
years' worth of canned goods . . . you know,
just in case of . . . armageddon.)

how old is edna? no one, including the
courthouse, knows. we assume it's somewhere
between sixty and eighty. let's just say
she doesn't look a day over whatever age
she claims to be.

leave it to the in-laws
to show up unannounced.

much like yourself,
christine enjoyed drama and was a queen.

i love it!
(what is it?)

it's perfect!
(what were they thinking?)

it's just what i wanted!
(i hope they saved the receipt!)

my summer vacation was fun.

we went to the washington monument.

my sister got cramps.

my brother lost his retainer.

mom cried a lot.

dad took us to an orphanage.

two words . . . night mare.

why? we scrimp and save all year long to take the family somewhere. washington, orlando, the alamo . . .

remember the six of you piling in the station wagon? (backed into the driveway for easy morning departure.) first bobby got carsick. susan left her retainer at the truck stop café. david whined about bobby vomiting on his paper where he had written down all the states for the license plate game. annie thought everything sucked because she was missing cheerleading camp. (mom had a purse full of liquor minis that were whittled down to nothing somewhere between the badlands and eureka springs.)

the only person smiling ear to ear was dad. he had the whole family together and twelve rolls of film. (get ready for the three-hour "summer of '69" slide presentation)

nadine . . . that wig looks fabulous!
but, how does it work on linoleum?